Story by: Calum Greenall
Illustrations by: Ellie Lewis
Published by: Eddie Hall
Design and Editing: Chris Stead, Old Mate Media
www.oldmatemedia.com

For orders and more info, please visit:
www.EddieHallStrongman.com

ISBN Paperback: 978-1-0687740-0-3
ISBN Hardcover: 978-1-0687740-1-0
ISBN Digital: 978-1-0687740-2-7

Remember boys and girls,
to always do your curls!
Big love, **THE BEAST!**

They call this man **THE BEAST**,
his real name's Eddie Hall.
He's The World's Strongest Man.
The strongest of them all!

When people see **THE BEAST**,
their jaws crash to the floor.
His muscles are so big,
they look at him with awe.

He can lift a whole house!

He can juggle three cars!

He can lift a large cow
and throw it up to **MARS!**

BEAST
CASTLE
He lives in
BEAST CASTLE,
the perfect home
for him.
WELCOME TO
BEAST CASTLE

A kitchen extra-large
and a super-sized gym!
Height of
average adult
human
BUTTER
MILK
MILK
MILK
MILK

It's tricky for THE BEAST, to live like me and you.
Just normal daily things are hard for him to do.
He can't find clothes that fit...
...he can't squeeze through a door.

He eats a hundred eggs
and still has room for more!

The worst thing for **THE BEAST**
is when he has to poo.
If he sits down too quick
his bum will break the...

LOO!

But **THE BEAST** doesn't mind,
he loves being super-strong.
He uses it for good
and tries to do no wrong.

DETROIT

The circus was in town,
a challenge extra tough:
THE GOLDEN WEIGHT OF DOOM!
THERE'S NO ONE STRONG ENOUGH!

COME AND TEST YOUR MUSCLES
AND SEE IF YOU CAN WIN!
"I'll see you there tonight!"
THE BEAST said with a grin.
CIRCUS
d' Magique
CAN YOU LIFT
THE GOLDEN WEIGHT
OF DOOM?
Come and test your strength
TONIGHT

The circus was just great, it really was a sight.
The crowd all "ooh'd" and "aah'd" as acrobats took flight!
Oooh!
Ahhh!

Then magic filled the tent!
A smoky flash and boom!
The final act before
THE GOLDEN WEIGHT
OF DOOM.

She made a little boy completely disappear!

And from **THE BEAST** she pulled, a hot dog from his ear!

"And for my final trick!"
said **THE GREAT TERESA**,
"I will make appear the...
Leaning Tower of Pisa!"

"Please, I must have silence.
The risk is very real."

But as she waved
her wand,
to make her
big reveal…

A clown trod on a horn, which went off with a HONK!
Honk!

His balls flew in the air and landed with a **BONK!**

The Tower had appeared,
but toppled to the side!
The crowd all froze in shock,
then… "HELP!" Teresa cried!

THE BEAST knew what to do!
He braced himself and pushed!
With super human strength, he
stopped them all being crushed!

The muscles **THE BEAST** had
were simply off the chart,
"But" she said, "your true strength
is held within your heart."

Each of the circus acts
came out and thanked THE BEAST.
Asking him to join them
for their end of show feast.

And then they watched him eat...
AND EAT... AND EAT... AND EAT!
'Til he'd gobbled so much
he was stuck in his seat!
Munch!
Crunch!

"Don't worry," said THE BEAST,
with a big cheeky grin.

Grrrrrr!

He bent his knees and arms,
then strained and tucked his chin...

BOOM!
THE BEAST let rip a fart so big the chair went BOOM!

It even lifted up
The Golden Weight of Doom!

The others coughed and choked;
their eyes were turning pink!

But **THE BEAST** didn't mind,
he loved his super-stink!

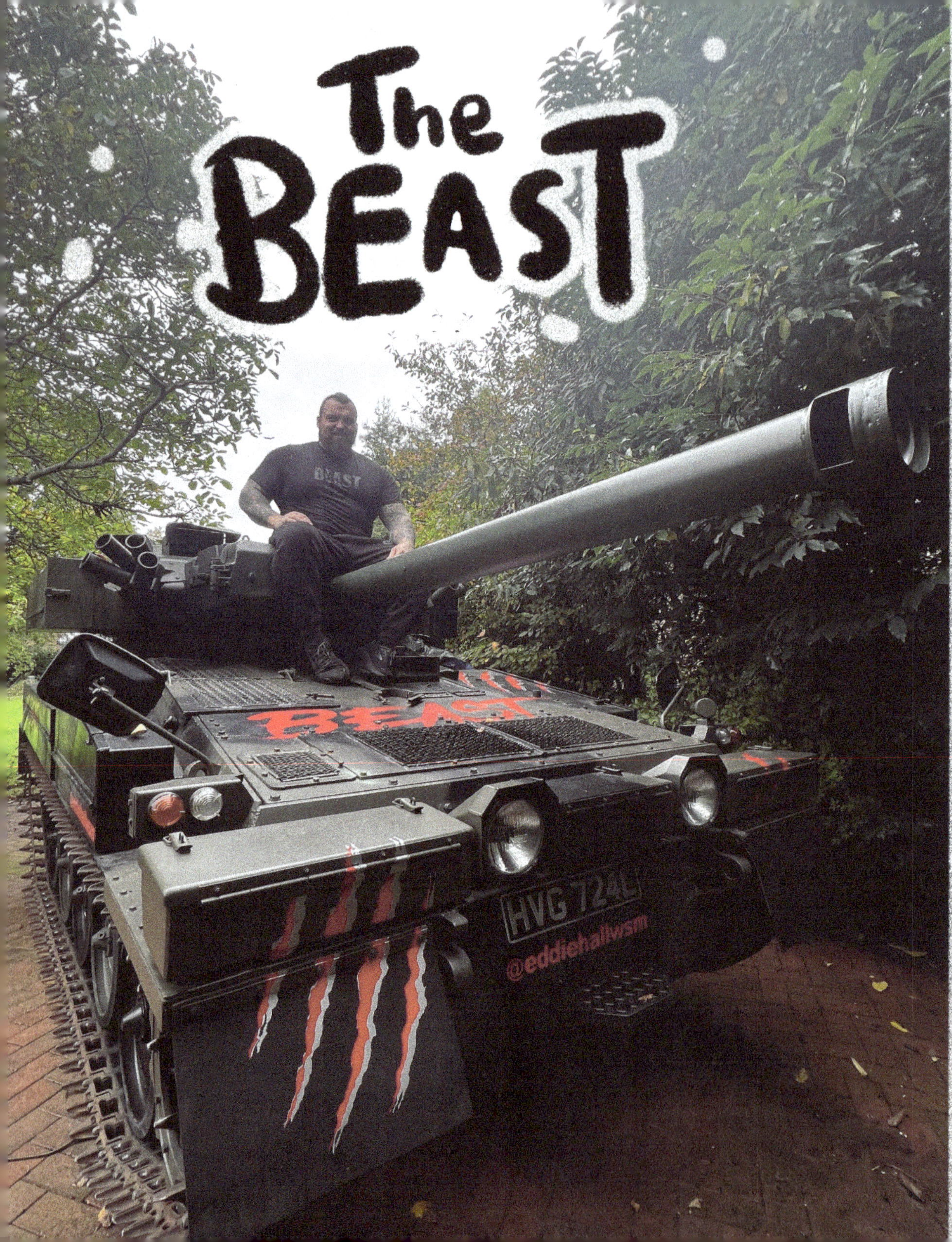
The BEAST
BEAST
BEAST
HVG 724L
@eddiehallwsm

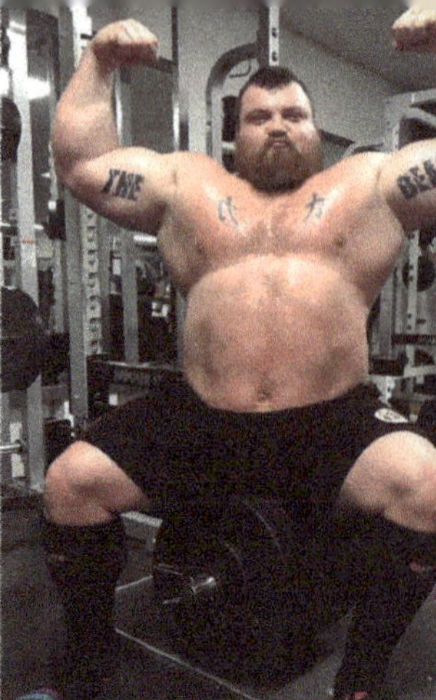

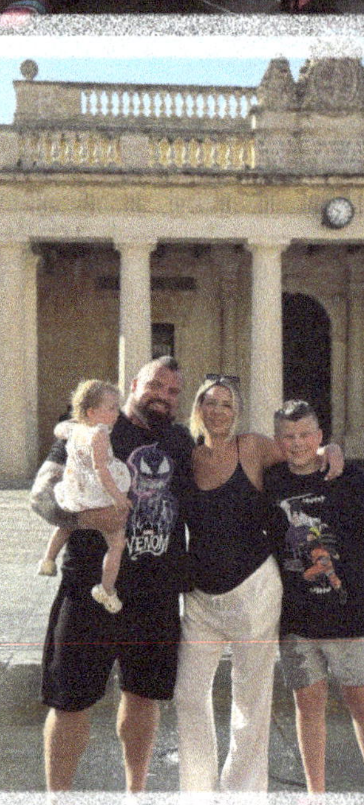

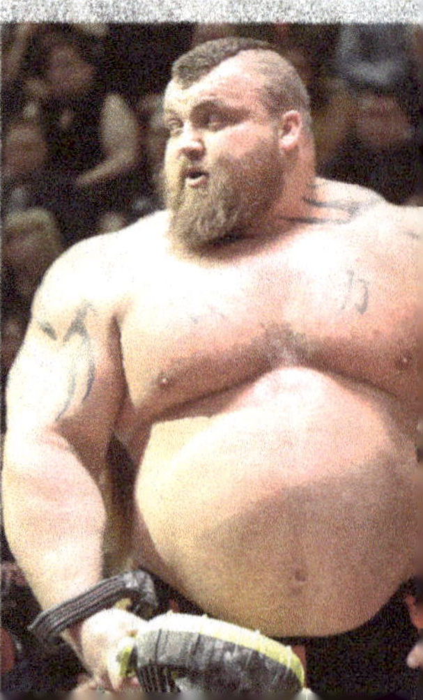

Eddie 'The Beast' Hall is a six-time UK's Strongest Man, the first person ever to dead lift 500kg (half a ton) and in 2017 he fulfilled his dream of becoming the World's Strongest Man!

Since then, he has gone on to be a boxer, MMA fighter, businessman, movie star and YouTube sensation! Eddie uses his media presence to both entertain and inspire.

When he's not in the gym, Eddie can be found driving around his hometown in his 20ton tank and spending quality time with his beautiful family.

And he really does love the smell of his own farts!